Instant Vortex Pro Air Fryer Oven Cookbook For Beginners

A Practical And Effective Cookbook To Effortless and Mouth-watering Instant Vortex Air Fryer Oven Recipes For The Family and friends

Martha Brown

Table of Contents

INTRODUCTION..8

CHAPTER 1. AIR FRYER GUIDELINES 10

1.4. BENEFITS OF THE AIR FRYER 11

CHAPTER 2: GRILL RECIPES...12

1.   CIDER BRINED PORK LOIN 12

2.   CHINESE SPARE RIBS 15

3.   CHICKEN FRIED CAULIFLOWER STEAK.................................17

4.   STUFFED ZUCCHINI CAPS...21

5.   VEGETABLE SUPREME PAN PIZZA 24

CHAPTER 3. BREAKFAST RECIPES 26

6.   CRUSTY BREAD...26

7.   EMPANADAS MINI SAUSAGES 27

CHAPTER 4. FAST FOOD RECIPES 28

8.   HOT DOGS...28

9.   TACO DOGS 29

CHAPTER 5. APPETIZERS AND SNACK RECIPES 32

10.   SALT AND VINEGAR CHICKPEAS...32

11.   BUFFALO-RANCH CHICKPEAS...34

12.   BAJA FISH TACO RECIPE 36

13.   LIGHTEN UP EMPANADAS 39

CHAPTER 6. CHICKEN AND TURKEY RECIPES 42

14.   SPICY AND CRISPY CHICKEN WING DRUMETTES..................42

15.   AIR-FRIED CHICKEN DRUMETTES 45

16. SPICY DRUMSTICKS WITH BARBECUE MARINADE 48

17. SOUTHERN CHICKEN DRUMSTICKS 50

18. NANDO'S CHICKEN DRUMSTICKS 53

19. COCONUT AND TURMERIC CHICKEN 56

CHAPTER 7. LAMB RECIPES **58**

20. ROASTED RACK OF LAMB WITH A MACADAMIA CRUST 58

CHAPTER 8. BEEF RECIPES **60**

21. STEAK IN THE AIR-FRYER 60

22. COUNTRY FRIED STEAK 62

CHAPTER 9. PORK RECIPES **64**

23. AIR-FRIED PORK DUMPLINGS WITH DIPPING SAUCE 64

CHAPTER 10. FISH RECIPES **68**

24. FISH AND CHIPS 68

25. FISH FINGERS 71

CHAPTER 11. SEAFOOD RECIPES **74**

26. CRISPY NACHOS PRAWNS 74

27. SCAMPI SHRIMP AND CHIPS 76

28. GAMBAS 'PIL PIL' WITH SWEET POTATO 79

29. FRIED HOT PRAWNS WITH COCKTAIL SAUCE 81

30. CRISPY AIR-FRYER COCONUT PRAWNS 83

CHAPTER 12. HOME BAKERY RECIPES **86**

31. CORNISH PASTY RECIPE 86

CHAPTER 13. RICE RECIPES **90**

32. STICKY MUSHROOM RICE 90

CHAPTER 14. BEANS AND LEGUMES RECIPES 92

33.   FALAFEL.. 92

CHAPTER 15. PASTA RECIPES 96

34.   MACCARONI AND CHEESE MINI QUICHE RECIPE................................. 96

CHAPTER 16. POTATO RECIPES 98

35.   GARLIC AND PARSLEY BABY POTATOES.. 98

CHAPTER 17. VEGETABLES 100

36.   BUTTERNUT SQUASH ROASTIES 100

37.   AVOCADO FRIES 102

39.   AIR FRIED GUACAMOLE... 105

CHAPTER 18: DESSERT RECIPES... 110

40.   CHOCOLATE CUPCAKES WITH CREAM CHEESE FROSTING RECIPE 110

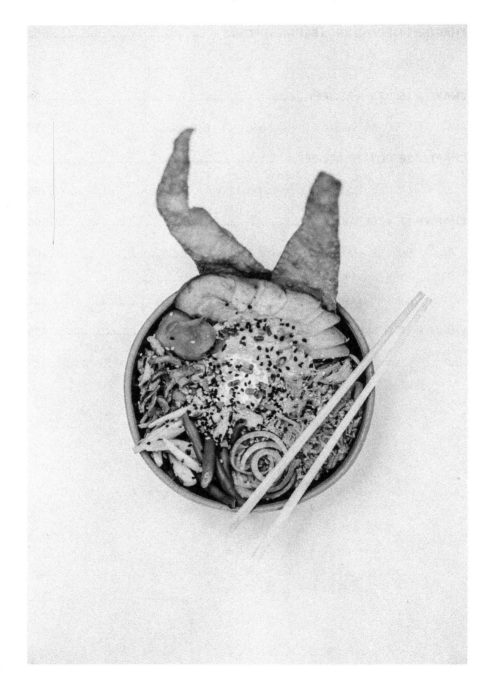

Introduction

All equipment should have flexibility, and that is deliberate as the supreme standard. In the unit, 7 times more high-temperature air is integrated. To facilitate its cooking feature, it offers additional accessories such as a non-stick griddle, a baking tray, a drip tray and a stainless-steel frying bowl. It has production output for up to 5 years.

Cleaning the air fryer is more than super easy, unlike most air fryers. It popped up with good dishwasher bits. It is made from stainless steel, so you can clean it easily. If you clean it regularly, it can last a long time and still be the perfect cooking quality.

The appliance comes with a 450-degree non-stick skillet that gives the barbecue an authentic stain and Taste.

This electric grill can quickly make the food crispier as compared to a conventional oven. Offering 7x superheated air, this electric grill. It has a 4-inch-long power cord.

The Air Fryer Grill is supplied with a handful of additional features, such as a non-stick griddle, baking dish, drip pan, and stainless-steel mesh fry basket.

One such powerful electric air fryer gives you a massive cooking room that allows you to cook 10-pound chicken, six huge burgers, and more.

For every cooking activity, this electric deep fryer grill rarely uses a lot of oil to make the ideal burgers and juicy, crispy fries with wings; instead, it lets you get 70 percent less calories for all these snacks.

Chapter 1. Air Fryer Guidelines

Air Fryer is a modern innovation among many other kitchen appliances. Although several individuals have already gotten accustomed to the air fryer as one of their favorite kitchen gadgets, several hundred individuals are still unaware of this new technology.

Why is Air Fryer outstanding?

It is important to regard an air fryer's cooking process as the unique elements of the gadget. For instance, most of the kitchenware was designed to use the conduction technique to produce foods; while, an air fryer is developed to use Convection – or airflow – for its cooking procedure.

An air fryer will fast and efficiently get your meals completed with a small amount of oil while using Rapid Air Technology.

An air fryer is made of:

1. Cooking chamber

This chamber is where the entire operation, including making the meal ready, takes place. Although the concept of function remains the same, depending on whether your model is constructed from a single tray or multiple layers of a tray, a cooking chamber's usability may differ.

2. Heating Element

The amount of heat needed to mix up with the moving air is calculated in this part. One of the most cherished virtues of the heating element of an Air Fryer is that it turns off automatically until the appropriate temperature required for cooking has been ascertained – this feature saves power and curbs unnecessary excessive heat.

3. Fan and Grill

This duo works together to ensure that the superheated air is uniformly distributed to the meal. The way the grill is built causes the airflow to be changed, which is an important component of the entire cooking activity.

4. Exhaust System

This mechanism is designed to help maintain an internal equilibrium pressure and block toxic air from accumulating. With a filter that eliminates the dust and any residual contaminants to clean the exhausted air, you can get some models. There will be no emission of an unwanted odor when doing this.

5. Movable Food Tray

The trays are specifically designed to transfer food that is to be cooked. Some models have a few border walls on the plate, allowing various meals to be cooked simultaneously. You can also get a model of any brand with a universal handle that can be used easily to extract the tray from the heating chamber.

1.4. Benefits of the Air Fryer

Air Fryer Outstanding advantages

- You can prepare healthy fast foods with air fryers better than those cooked with the standard frying technique.

- It's easy to use.

- It needs low maintenance, and washing is easy.

- Over a relatively brief time, the air fryer cooks food.

- In terms of protection, it is safer to use.

Chapter 2: Grill Recipes

1. Cider Brined Pork Loin

Prep + Cook Time: 30 minutes | Servings: 2

Ingredients:

- 4 thyme sprigs

- 3 tablespoon sugar

- 2 cup Brown Sugar

- 1/2 teaspoon red pepper flakes

- 3.5 cup apple cider vinegar

- 3/4 cup Kosher Salt

- 3 cup water

- 3 tablespoon Honey

- 1 tablespoon mustard seeds

- 1 teaspoon horseradish

- 1 tablespoon black peppercorns

- 1 teaspoon horseradish

- 1/3 cup Dijon mustard

- 3-pound pork loin

Directions:

1. In a bowl to make the dressing, horseradish, Dijon mustard, sugar and honey altogether. Store the bowl aside.

2. In a shallow skillet to prepare the brine, combine the mustard seeds, pepper sugar, salt, peppercorns, and 2 cups of apple cider vinegar, flakes, thyme and 1 tablespoon of horseradish. Take it to a boil with the ingredients.

3. Remove the soup from the heat. For 30 minutes, let the ingredients relax.

4. In a saucepan, add 11/2 cups of apple cider vinegar and water.

5. Marinate the pork in the brine for 12 hours until the brine has cooled completely. With paper towels, wipe the pork off.

6. With the dressing, coat the bacon.

7. With the Rotisserie Forks and Set Screws, place the pork on the Rotisserie Shaft and secure the shaft. Set the Shaft into the Rotisserie Shaft slots of the appliance.

8. To raise the cooking time to 60 minutes, press the Power Button and then the Rotisserie Button (400° F). When the pork is frying, brush the mixture over the pork every 15 minutes.

9. Pick out the pork carefully using the Fetch Tool.

2. Chinese Spare Ribs

Prep + Cook Time: 20-30 minutes | Servings: 2

Ingredients:

- 1 tablespoon sake

- 1/2 teaspoon rice vinegar

- 1 tablespoon sweet chili sauce

- 2-pound boneless pork spare ribs

- 1/4 teaspoon salt

- 1 tablespoon Honey

- 1 clove Garlic

- 1/4 teaspoon Chinese five-spice powder

- 2 tablespoon ketchup

- 1 teaspoon ginger

- 2 tablespoon Hoisin sauce

Directions:

1. In a bowl, bring the marinade ingredients together and stir.

2. Pour the marinade over ribs and marinade for half an hour.

3. Thread two skewers with the ribs.

4. With the Rotisserie Shaft, set up the Flexible Skewer Racks and cover the Shaft with the Rotisserie Forks and Set Screws.

5. In the Adjustable Skewer Racks, bolt each of the skewers. Set Racks in the Rotisserie Shaft sockets of the appliance.

6. To raise the cooking time to 40 minutes, press the Power Button and then the Rotisserie Button (400° F). Brush the ribs every 10 minutes with the marinade while the ribs are cooking.

7. With the Fetch Tool, softly erase the ribs.

3. Chicken Fried Cauliflower Steak

Prep + Cook Time: 30 minutes | Servings: 2

Ingredients:

- 2 teaspoons Paprika

- 1/2 cup vegetable stock

- 1 teaspoon Sea Salt

- 1/4 Onion

- 1 tablespoon Dijon mustard

- 6 White Mushrooms

- 2 large eggs

- 1 vegetable bouillon cube

- 1/2 tablespoon Garlic powder

- 1 large cauliflower head

- 1/2 stick butter

- 1/4 cup buttermilk

- Olive oil spray

- 3/2 cup whole milk

- 1/4 teaspoon cayenne pepper

- 1/2 tablespoon onion powder

- 1 clove Garlic

- 1 cup flour

- 2 tablespoon water

Directions:

1. Break the cauliflower into 3/4-inch steaks.

2. On 2 Air Flow Racks, put the cauliflower. Place the Power Air Fryer Oven Racks on the bottom and middle shelves.

3. To reduce the cooking time to 10 minutes, press the power button and then the baking button (350 ° F).

4. Allow 10 minutes for the cauliflower to cool.

5. Mix the ingredients in a bowl with the flour mixture.

6. In another bowl, put together the ingredients for the egg mixture.

7. Dip the egg mixture with the cauliflower and then the flour blend. Place aside the remaining flour mixture.

8. Place it on a rack with the cauliflower. Spray the olive oil with the cauliflower. Place the rack on the appliance's middle shelf.

9. To reduce the cooking time to 10 minutes, press the Power Button and then the French Fries Button (400° F).

10. In a saucepan over medium heat, melt the butter and sauté the onions, garlic, and mushrooms until they are tender.

11. Add 3 tbsp. flour mixture to the sauté pan and whisk the mixture until the flour is immersed.

12. Include the sauce ingredients to the sauté pan and mix the pan until creamy. Cook until you reach the desired thickness.

13. Include the cauliflower in the sauce, eventually.

4. Stuffed Zucchini Caps

Prep + Cook Time: 40 minutes | Servings: 2

Ingredients:

- 1/2 cup carrot

- 1/4 teaspoon ground fennel seed

- 1 oregano sprig

- 1/4 cup Red bell pepper

- 1/4 cup plain breadcrumbs

- 3 tablespoon butter

- 2 medium zucchinis

- 1 pinch freshly ground black pepper

- 1/4 teaspoon Sea Salt

- 2 sweet sausages

- 1/4 cup shredded mozzarella

- 1/4 cup Onion

Directions:

1. Take out the sausages from their casings.

2. Place the sausages on an air-flow rack. Place the rack on the middle shelf of the Power Air Fryer.

3. Click the Control Button (at 370 degree for 15 minutes).

4. Take out the sausages and slice them into little pieces.

5. Expose the interior of the zucchini, leaving the outside with a crust.

6. Slice off the pulp of the zucchini.

7. Melt the butter in a saucepan over medium-high heat and sauté the onion, fennel seeds, zucchini pulp, red pepper, carrot, and bits of sausage until tender.

8. For 2 minutes, cook the oregano, breadcrumbs, ground black pepper and sea salt over medium heat.

9. Add the mozzarella to the prepared mixture and blend fully. Use the cooked mixture to serve each zucchini hat.

10. To place the stuffed zucchinis, use two shelves. The racks are located on the bottom and middle shelves of the appliance.

11. Press the power button and then the baking button (350° F) to reduce the cooking time to 15 minutes.

5. Vegetable Supreme Pan Pizza

Prep + Cook Time: 20-30 minutes | Servings: 2

Ingredients:

- 8 slice White Onion

- 12 slice Tomato

- 2 tablespoon olive oil

- 3/2 cup shredded mozzarella

- 8 Cremini mushrooms

- 1/2 green pepper

- 4 tablespoon Pesto

- 1 Pizza Dough

- 1 cup spinach

Directions:

Roll the pizza dough halves until they each meet the size of the Air Flow racks.

Grease all sides of each dough lightly with olive oil.

On a rack, put each pizza. Place the racks on the electric fryer's upper and lower shelves.

Then press the power button and the cooking time to 13 minutes by pressing the French Fries button (400-degree F).

Flip the dough onto the top shelf after 5 minutes and switch the racks.Switch the dough on to the top shelf after 4 minutes. Take both racks out and drizzle the toppings with the pizzas. Place the racks on the electric fryer's upper and lower shelves.

Then push the power button and the cooking time to 7 minutes by pressing the French Fries button (400-degree F).

Rotate the pizzas after 4 minutes. If the pizzas are done, let them rest before cutting them for 4 minutes.

Chapter 3. Breakfast Recipes

6. Crusty Bread

Prep + Cook time: 8-10 minutes | Servings: 2

Ingredients:

- Stale or baked and frozen loaves of bread (various types)

- Sufficient water

Directions:

1. At the bottom of the container, scatter the loaves of bread and sprinkle a little water.

2. Select 400-degree F, close the lid and set the time to 6 minutes.

3. Then serve the newly flavored crispy bread.

7. Empanadas Mini Sausages

Prep + Cook time: 10-11 minutes | Servings: 20

Ingredients:

- ½ lb. mini sausages

- 3 ½ oz. puff pastry already prepared (refrigerated or frozen, thawed) - 1 tbsp. of mustard powder

Directions:-Preheat to 400-degree F with the fryer. Completely drain the sausages and gently pat dry on a sheet of paper towels.Break the puff pastry into strips of 5 x 11⁄2 cm and put a thin layer of powdered mustard over the strips. Wrap a spiral strip of dough for each sausage.In the basket, put half the sausages covered in batter and slip them into the fryer.For 10-11 minutes, set the timer. Bake until golden brown with the breaded sausages. In the same way, cook the leftover sausages. Serve the sausages, followed by a cup of mustard on a plate.

Chapter 4. Fast Food Recipes

8. Hot Dogs

Prep + Cook Time: 12 minutes | Servings: 2

Ingredients:

- 2 hot dogs

- 2 hot dog buns

- 2 tbsp. of grated cheese, optional

Directions:

Ensure the air fryer is preheated for approximately 4 minutes at 390-degree F.In an air fryer, cook the two hot dogs for about 5 minutes, then cut them.Place the hot dog in a bun, and you should add cheese.Place the dressed hot dog back in the air fryer and let it steam for an additional 2 minutes.

9. Taco Dogs

Prep + Cook Time: 17 minutes | Servings: 2

Ingredients:

- 2 jumbo hot dogs

- 1 tsp taco seasoning mix

- 2 hot dog buns

- 1/3 cup guacamole

- 4 tbsp. salsa

- 6 pickled jalapeno slices

Directions:

1. Make sure that the air fryer is preheated for at least four minutes at 390-degree F.

2. On each hot dog, cut five slits and sprinkle 1/2 teaspoon of taco seasoning on each hot dog.

3. Allow the hot dogs to cook for about 5 minutes in the air fryer before they are placed on the bus and back in the air fryer basket.

4. Cook until the buns are toasted and the hot dogs are crispy this time around. This takes 4 minutes or so or so.

5. Top the hot dogs, all in equal amounts, with guacamole, salsa and jalapenos

Chapter 5. Appetizers and Snack Recipes

10.Salt and Vinegar Chickpeas

Prep + Cook Time: 55 minutes | Servings: 2

Ingredients:

- 1 (15 oz.) can chickpeas, drained and rinsed

- 1 cup white vinegar

- ½ tsp sea salt

- 1 tbsp. olive oil

Directions:

1. Get a clean small saucepan, and in it, combine chickpeas and vinegar. Bring to a simmer over high heat. Once simmering, withdraw and allow to stand for 30 minutes.

2. Drain the chickpeas and get rid of all loose skins.

3. Ensure that your air fryer is preheated to 390-degree F.

4. With the chickpeas spread evenly in the air fryer basket, allow cooking for about 4 minutes or until the chickpeas dry out.

5. Move the dried chickpeas into a heat-proof bowl. Drizzle with sea salt and oil and stir to coat evenly.

6. Place the coated chickpeas into the air fryer again and allow cooking for about 8 minutes. Endeavor to shake the basket at 2- or 3-minutes intervals. Remove once you have lightly browned chickpeas.

7. Serve instantly.

11. Buffalo-Ranch Chickpeas

Prep + Cook Time: 35 minutes | Servings: 2

Ingredients:

- 1 (15 oz.) can chickpeas, drained and rinsed

- 2 tbsp. Buffalo wing sauce

- 1 tbsp. dry ranch dressing mix

Directions:

1. Ensure that your air fryer is preheated to 350-degree F.

2. After lining your baking sheet with paper towels, spread the chickpeas over the lined paper towels. Cover the chickpeas with another layer of paper towels, and press gently to drain any excess moisture.

3. Place the chickpeas in a bowl and pour in the wing sauce. Stir the mixture to combine.

4. Add ranch dressing powder and mix well to combine.

5. Arrange the air fryer in an even layer in the air fryer basket.

6. Allow cooking for 8 minutes. Stop, shake, and cook for an extra 5 minutes, shake again, and cook for 5 minutes more, and shake again for the last time before cooking for the final 2 minutes.

7. Set aside the cooked chickpeas for about 5 minutes to allow cooling.

8. Serve immediately.

12.Baja Fish Taco Recipe

Prep + Cook Time: 40 minutes | Servings: 4

Ingredients:

- 1 red onion

- 1 large mango

- 7 oz. fresh cod fillet

- Salt and ground black pepper to taste

- 2 tbsp. coriander

- 1 tbsp. cumin

- 8 tbsp. Mexican seasoning

- 2 medium eggs

- 1 tbsp. garlic puree

- 2 tbsp. quark

- 4 limes

- 5 oz. gluten-free oats

- 4 homemade tortilla wraps

Directions:

1. Chop them into small pieces after peeling the red onion and mango, and set them aside.

2. Clean the fresh cod and cut it into bits that are easy to bite. In addition to half the coriander, apply salt and pepper generously.

3. Get a large mixing bowl and mix both the seasonings and the other half of the cilantro together in it. Also, add 3/4 of the previously chopped red onion, the eggs, and the garlic. To blend, balance well. Toss in the quark and stir in the juice and 3 out of 4 limes with the rind. To shape a smooth batter, blend thoroughly again.

4. In a blender, put 3/4 of the oats and blend until you have a mixture like fine breadcrumbs. Before tossing in the new

cod, combine the paste with unblended oats and blend well. Ensure that the new cod in the oat mixture is well coated.

5. Transfer the battered cod parts into the grill pan of the air fryer, and cook at 365 F for 10 minutes.

6. Cover and shake before cooking at 390-degree F for an additional 3 minutes.

7. Toss the fried fish into the wraps that have just been cooked. Apply the combination of the mango and red onion as the toppings.

8. Along with salt and pepper, apply some lime juice from the remaining lime as a seasoning.

9. Just serve.

13.Lighten up Empanadas

Prep + Cook Time: 50 minutes | Servings: 2

Ingredients:

- 1 tbsp. olive oil

- 3 oz. lean ground beef

- ¼ cup white onion, chopped

- 3 oz. Cremini mushrooms, chopped

- 6 pitted green olives, chopped

- ¼ tsp ground cumin

- 2 tsp garlic, chopped

- ¼ tsp paprika

- 1/8 tsp ground cinnamon

- ½ cup tomatoes, chopped

- 8 square gyoza wrappers

- 1 large egg, lightly beaten

Directions:

1. Get a medium, clean skillet and add some oil in.

2. Medium-high heat.

3. Toss in the beef and onion, and allow to cook to crumble when stirring. After 3 minutes, or when the beef and onion start to brown, avoid cooking.

4. Add the mushrooms and, while stirring regularly, finish cooking. Stop cooking after 6 minutes or when the brown mushrooms surface.

5. Now toss in the olives, cumin, garlic, paprika, and cinnamon and simmer until the mushrooms are very tender and moisture-free. This will take about 3 minutes.

6. Attach the tomatoes and simmer, stirring intermittently, for another minute.

7. In a clean bowl, pass the filling and set aside to cool for about 5 minutes.

8. Carefully arrange four gyoza wrappers on the work table. Pour approximately 1.5 teaspoons of filling into the middle of each wrapper. Now, clean the sides of the wrapper with an egg and fold each one over. Seal the corners by pinching.

9. For the other wrappers and the filling, do the same.

10. Arrange four empanadas in a single sheet of your air-fryer basket. Cook for 7 minutes at 400-degree F or until well browned.

11. For the other empanadas, do the same.

Chapter 6. Chicken and Turkey Recipes

14.Spicy and Crispy Chicken Wing Drumettes

Prep + Cook Time: 40 minutes | Servings: 2

Ingredients:

- 10 large chicken wing Drumettes

- Cooking spray

- 1 tbsp. soy sauce

- 3/8 tsp red pepper, crushed

- 2 tbsp. chicken stock, unsalted

- 1 clove garlic, chopped

- ¼ cup rice vinegar

- 1 tbsp. toasted sesame oil

- 3 tbsp. honey

- 2 tbsp. roasted peanuts, unsalted and chopped

- 1 tbsp. fresh chives, chopped

Directions:

1. Ensure the heating process of the Air Fryer to 400-degree F.

2. Arrange the Drumettes on the sides of the chicken in the air fryer basket for increased space management.

3. Spray them with cooking spray while they are in the basket.

4. Until turning, on the other hand, cause the sprayed chicken to cook for 15 minutes and cook for 15 minutes again.

5. In a clean skillet, prepare a mixture of soy sauce, red pepper, chicken stock, garlic, rice vinegar, sesame oil and honey.

6. Stir and bring the honey sauce till it simmers, using medium-height heat. The sauce will appear slightly thickened. Then boil for 6 minutes.

7. In a clean dish, place the fried chicken wings and apply the honey sauce, then stir mildly.

8. Sprinkle with peanuts and chopped chives until the wings are well seasoned.

9. Just serve.

15.Air-Fried Chicken Drumettes

Prep + Cook Time: 30 minutes | Servings: 2-4

Ingredients:

- 1½ lbs. chicken wing Drumettes

- Olive oil cooking spray

- 1 tbsp. lower-sodium soy sauce

- ½ tsp cornstarch

- 1 tsp finely chopped garlic

- ½ tsp finely chopped fresh ginger

- 1 tsp Sambal Oelek (ground fresh chili paste)

- 1/8 tsp kosher salt

- 1 tsp fresh lime juice

- 2 tsp honey

- 2 tbsp. chopped scallions

Directions:

1. Using paper towels, pat the rinsed chicken Drumettes dry and then brush with olive oil.

2. Make sure the air fryer is preheated to 400-degree F.

3. Transfer the chicken Drumettes, keeping a single coat, to the air fryer.

4. Allow the air fryer to cook for 22 minutes, shaking two or three times.

5. When crispy, withdraw the Drumettes.

6. Take a clean saucepan and mix the soy sauce and cornstarch with the Drumettes in your air fryer.

7. Place the garlic, the ginger, the Sambal, the salt, the lime juice and the honey together.

8. Thoroughly swirl the blend and move to medium-high pressure.

9. Cook until the mixture has thickened and bubbles start to form.

10. Remove the Drumettes from the chicken and put them in a big bowl.

11. Over the Drumettes, pour the sauce mixture and stir mildly.

12. Before eating, add chopped scallions and toppings.

16.Spicy Drumsticks with Barbecue Marinade

Prep + Cook Time: 45 minutes | Servings: 4

Ingredients:

- 1 tsp chili powder

- 2 tsp brown sugar

- 1 clove garlic, crushed

- ½ tbsp. mustard

- A pinch of salt

- Freshly ground black pepper

- 1 tbsp. olive oil

- 4 drumsticks

Directions:

1. Ensure that the air fryer is preheated to 390-degree F.

2. Create a mixture of chili powder, brown sugar, garlic, mustard, and add a pinch of salt and freshly ground pepper to taste.

3. Add oil to this mixture, stir.

4. Do a thorough rubbing of the drumsticks, using the marinade and allow the rubbed sticks to marinate for 20 minutes.

5. Now, place the drumsticks in the basket, and put the basket into the Air Fryer, allowing it to roast for 10 minutes or until they are brown.

5. Drop the air fryer temperature to 300-degree F and allow them to roast for additional 10 minutes.

6. Remove the roasted drumsticks and serve with French bread and corn salad.

17.Southern Chicken Drumsticks

Prep + Cook Time: 55 minutes | Servings: 4

Ingredients:

- 2 large slices of bread

- Salt and ground black pepper to taste

- 1 tbsp. dried garlic and onion

- 1 tsp basil

- ½ tsp cayenne pepper

- 1 tbsp. plain flour

- 2 tbsp. paprika

- 5 oz. buttermilk

- 4 chicken drumsticks

- 1 tbsp. oregano

- 1 tbsp. rosemary

- 1 tbsp. thyme

- 1 tsp olive oil

Directions:

1. Ensure that it takes only two minutes to preheat the Air Fryer to about 365 F.

2. Add salt, pepper, dried garlic, tomato, basil, and a touch of cayenne in addition to the bread. In the mixer, combine the mixture until the mixture looks like breadcrumbs. Place the mixture in a different bowl and set it aside.

3. Add the flour to a new bowl and mix with 1/2 of the paprika and add the pepper and salt to taste. Set this bowl aside, too, though.

4. Get the third bowl of buttermilk, chicken drumsticks, and the rest of the seasonings and make a mixture. Stir the mixture well when submerging the drumsticks.

5. Take each chicken drumstick out of the bowl and placed it in the flour and in the breadcrumbs after that.

6. If the dipping for each one is complete, place them in your air fryer in the basket.

7. Sprinkle a bit of olive oil after covering all the chicken drumsticks to ensure that they do not dry, thus enhancing their flavor.

8. Place all the coated and oiled drumsticks in the fryer and cook at 365 F for approximately 30 minutes. Drop the heat to 345-degree F and simmer for an additional two minutes.

9. Remove the fryer from the air and serve.

18.Nando's Chicken Drumsticks

Prep + Cook Time: 35 minutes | Servings: 4

Ingredients:

- 2 corn on the cobs

- 1 small fresh red chili

- ½ bunch of fresh parsley, chopped

- 1 tsp paprika

- 5 garlic cloves, peeled

- 3 bay leaves

- 3 tbsp. olive oil

- 8 chicken drumsticks

- Salt and ground black pepper to taste

- ½ tsp Piri oiled seasoning

- 1 tsp butter

Directions:

1. On the cob, pick each corn and cut it into three equal pieces, making you six equal pieces of chopped maize. Put these bits into your Instant Pot's steamer bowl, which already has 1 cup of water under it. Seal the lid and allow the steamer button to cook for 15 minutes.

2. Add the red pepper, parsley, paprika, garlic, bay leaves, and olive oil to the blender. Blend, so you have a near-smooth or grainy blend.

3. Arrange the chicken drumsticks on a clean chopping board and drizzle salt and pepper over them. Brush each drumstick with the blended marinade with the help of your pastry brush.

4. Proceed by putting the brushed drumsticks in the air fryer's grill pan. Fix the temperature and cook for 12 minutes at 355-degree F.

5. Once you get a beep sound from the Instant Pot, use the Quick pressure release to extract the corn on the cob. Transfer it to the chopping board and, along with salt and pepper to taste, season with Piri oiled seasoning.

6. Set the temperature to 390-degree F and allow it to cook on the other side for an extra three minutes, plus the corn on the cob. This will give them the look of a well-done barbecue.

7. Before serving it with the Peri oiled chicken Drumettes, you can add a little butter to the corn on the cob.

19.Coconut and Turmeric Chicken

Prep + Cook Time: 4 hours 40 minutes | Servings: 2-3

Ingredients:

- 3 pcs whole chicken leg (de-skin or with skin is totally up to you)

- 4-5 tsp ground turmeric

- ½ tbsp. salt

- 2 oz. galangal

- 2 oz. pure coconut paste (or coconut milk)

- 2 oz. old ginger

Direction:

1. Do not pound or blend chicken meat; it should be pounded or blended with all of the other ingredients.

2. Cut a few slits on the leg of the chicken with an emphasis on the dense materials. During marinating, the cuttings can improve the absorption of the spice.

3. Add the mixed ingredients to the chicken and allow it to marinate for no less than four hours, or overnight if possible. The seasoned chicken should be wrapped with an adhesive film after the marinating process and kept inside the refrigerator.

4. Set the air fryer to 375-degree F and allow the chicken to preheat at this temperature, then fry the chicken for about 20-25 minutes, frying half of the total time on each hand.

5. Once you've got a golden-brown chicken, you can carry on eating.

Chapter 7. Lamb Recipes

20. Roasted Rack of Lamb with a Macadamia Crust

Prep + Cook Time: 45 minutes | Servings: 4

Ingredients:

- 1 garlic clove

- 1 tbsp. olive oil

- 2 lbs. rack of lamb

- Salt and ground black pepper to taste

- 3 oz. macadamia nuts, unsalted

- 1 tbsp. chopped fresh rosemary

- 1 tbsp. breadcrumbs (preferably homemade)

- 1 egg, beaten

Directions:

Make sure the air fryer is preheated to 210 F.To make the garlic oil, cut the garlic into fine pieces and mix them with oil. In addition to the garlic oil, season the lamb rack with salt and pepper.Chop the nuts thinly and place the pieces in a bowl and add the rosemary and breadcrumbs.Get a clean bowl and whisk in it the egg.In the egg mixture, dredge the meat and rinse off the excess. Again, dip it into the macadamia crust.

Shift the coated lamb rack to the basket of the air fryer and allow it to cook for 25 minutes.

Increase the temperature after 25 minutes to 390-degree F. Cook at 390-degree F for 5 minutes.

Remove from the air fryer and allow to rest and cover with aluminum foil for another 10 minutes.

Serve.

Chapter 8. Beef Recipes

21.Steak in the Air-fryer

Prep + Cook Time: 10 minutes | Servings: 2

Ingredients:

- Steak with a thickness of 1-inch

- Olive oil

- Salt and ground black pepper to taste

Directions:

1. Remove the steak from the fridge.

2. Insert your baking tray into the air fryer, and preheat it for about 5 minutes at 390-degree F.

3. Use your olive oil to coat the steak on either side generously.

4. Use your salt and pepper to season the steak on either side.

5. Transfer the steak into the air fryer's baking tray.

6. Allow cooking for 3 minutes.

7. Once the timer goes off, flip the steak to the other side and cook for another 3 minutes.

8. Transfer the cooked steak to a plate.

9. Let it cool for 3 minutes more before serving.

22. Country Fried Steak

Prep + Cook Time: 40 minutes | Servings: 1

Ingredients:

- 1 tsp garlic powder

- 1 tsp onion powder

- 1 tsp salt

- 1 tsp ground black pepper

- 1 cup Panko bread crumbs

- 6 oz. sirloin steak-pounded thin

- 1 cup flour

- 3 eggs, beaten

Sausage Gravy (optional):

- 6 oz. ground sausage meat

- 2 tbsp. flour

- 2 cups milk

- 1 tsp ground black pepper

Directions:

1. Season the panko by using the spices as a seasoning.

2. Dip the steak, respectively, in rice, egg and seasoned panko.

3. Transfer the dredged steak into the basket of the air fryer and close. Set the temperature to 370 F and give 12 minutes to cook.

4. After 12 minutes, remove the steak and serve with sausage gravy or potato mash.

Chapter 9. Pork Recipes

23. Air-Fried Pork Dumplings with Dipping Sauce

Prep + Cook Time: 1 hour 10 minutes | Servings: 6

Ingredients:

- 1 tsp canola oil

- 4 cups bok Choy (about 12 oz.), chopped

- 1 tbsp. garlic (3 garlic cloves), chopped

- 1 tbsp. fresh ginger, chopped

- 4 oz. ground pork

- ¼ tsp crushed red pepper

- 18 (3 1/2-inch-square) dumpling wrappers or wonton wrappers

- Cooking spray

- 2 tbsp. rice vinegar

- ½ tsp packed light brown sugar

- 1 tbsp. finely chopped scallions

- 1 tsp toasted sesame oil

- 2 tsp lower-sodium soy sauce

Directions:

1. Get a clean, large nonstick skillet and fire it over medium-high heat with your canola oil.

2. Add bok Choy and cook until the mixture is wilted and almost dry while stirring constantly. This takes about 6 to 8 minutes.

3. Toss throughout the garlic and ginger and cook for a minute again, this time stirring constantly.

4. Remove the mixture of bok Choy and put it in a bowl for 5 minutes. Pat the mixture dries with a paper towel.

5. Take a medium bowl and stir together the bok Choy combination, ground pork, and crushed red pepper in it.

6. Place a dumpling wrapper on your work surface and add one tablespoon of filling in the center of the wrapper using a spoon. To moisten the edges of the wrapper lightly with water, use your fingers or your pastry brush. To offer a half-moon shape, fold the wrapper over and tap the edges to seal. For the other wrappers and the filling, do the same.

7. Using the cooking oil, coat the air fryer basket lightly. In the basket, arrange six dumplings such that there is a little space for each one. With the cooking spray, spray the dumplings lightly.

8. Set the Air Fryer to 375-degree F and allow the dumplings to cook for 12 minutes until lightly browned. Halfway through frying, turn the dumplings over (at 6 minutes). While

keeping the cooked dumplings warm, do the same for all the dumplings.

9. Prepare a paste of rice vinegar, brown sugar, scallions, sesame oil, and soy sauce in a small bowl while cooking the dumplings. If the sugar is dissolved, stir together.

10. Serve by putting three dumplings alongside two teaspoons of sauce on each plate.

Chapter 10. Fish Recipes

24. Fish and Chips

Prep + Cook Time: 45 minutes | Servings: 4

Ingredi0ents:

- 2 (10 oz.) russet potatoes, scrubbed

- Cooking spray

- 1¼ tsp kosher salt, divided

- 1 cup (about 4¼ oz.) all-purpose flour

- 2 large eggs

- 2 tbsp. water

- 1 cup whole-wheat panko (Japanese-style breadcrumbs)

- 4 (6 oz.) skinless tilapia fillets

- ½ cup malt vinegar

Directions:

1. Use your spiralizer to cut the potatoes into spirals by following the manufacturer's guidance. Place each batch of spiral potatoes into the basket of the air fryer. Spray generously with cooking spray so that each piece is well coated.

2. Set the air fryer to 375-degree F and cook for 10 minutes of cooking (or until they are crispy and golden brown). Halfway into frying, turn the potatoes off. Transfer them into a separate dish, until baked, and cover to stay warm. For the other batches, do the same. Sprinkle 1/4 teaspoon of salt with all the fried potatoes.

3. Get a shallow dish and place your flour and add 1/2 teaspoon of salt as you cook the potatoes. In another small dish, lightly whisk the eggs and water together. Get a third

shallow dish and stir together the panko and the unused 1/2 teaspoon salt.

4. Lengthwise, cut each fish fillet into two long strips and dip each strip into the mixture of flour, egg mixture, and panko mixture, respectively. To coat the fish pieces on both sides, add the cooking spray.

5. Transfer the fish to the basket of the air fryer (in a single layer). Allow each batch to cook at 375-degree F for 10 minutes (or until golden brown). Remember to halfway through cooking to turn fish over.

6. Serve by placing on each plate two fish pieces alongside equal portions of potato spirals. For dipping, mix two tablespoons of malt vinegar.

25. Fish Fingers

Prep + Cook Time: 25 minutes | Servings: 2

Ingredients:

- 2 slices whole meal bread made into breadcrumbs

- Salt and ground black pepper to taste

- 1 tsp parsley

- 2 oz. plain flour

- 1 medium egg, beaten

- 2 white fish fillets skinned and boned

- 1 tsp mixed herbs

- 1 small lemon juice only

- 1 tsp thyme

Directions:

1. Ensure that your air fryer is preheated to 360-degree F.

2. To prepare your breadcrumbs, place them in a clean dish and mix it thoroughly with pepper, parsley, and salt. Transfer your beaten egg to a separate dish and the plain flour in another.

3. Place the fish in a food processor alongside mixed herbs, salt and pepper, lemon juice, and thyme. When the mixture is all mashed up like uncooked fishcakes, start making your fish fingers.

4. Bread your fish – roll it in the flour, the egg, and then in the breadcrumbs.

5. Transfer the rolled fish into the air fryer and allow to cook at 360-degree F for 8 minutes.

6. Serve the cooked rolled fish alongside potatoes and mayonnaise. You may also serve in a sandwich.

Chapter 11. Seafood Recipes

26. Crispy Nachos Prawns

Prep + Cook Time: 25 minutes | Servings: 6

Ingredients:

- 18 large prawns, peeled and deveined, tails left on

- 1 egg, beaten

- 1 (10 oz.) bag nacho-cheese flavored corn chips, finely crushed

Directions:

1. Rinse the prawns and dry by patting them.

2. Get a small bowl and whisk the egg in it. Transfer the crushed chips to a separate bowl.

3. Dip a prawn in the whisked egg and the crushed chips, respectively.

4. Transfer the coated prawn to a plate and do the same for the remaining prawns.

5. Ensure that your Air Fryer is preheated to 350-degree F.

6. Transfer the coated prawns into the air fryer and allow to cook for 8 minutes.

7. Opaque prawns mean they are well cooked.

8. Remove from the air fryer and serve.

27. Scampi Shrimp and Chips

Prep + Cook Time: 25 minutes | Servings: 4

Ingredients:

- 2 medium potatoes

- Salt and ground black pepper to taste

- 1 tbsp. olive oil

- 1 lb. King prawns

- 1 small egg

- 5 oz. gluten-free oats

- 1 large lemon

- 1 tsp thyme

- 1 tbsp. parsley

Directions:

1. Cut them into chunky chips after peeling the potatoes, then season with pepper and salt. Drizzle the chip with a little olive oil. Lastly, cook for 5 minutes at 360-degree F in an air fryer.

2. Rinse the prawns and rinse with a kitchen towel by patting them. To the chopping board, move them and season with pepper and salt.

3. Transfer the egg into a small bowl and blend until you have a beaten egg, using a fork.

4. In the blender, put 80 percent of the gluten-free oats alongside the thyme and parsley. Blend before a paste that looks like coarse breadcrumbs appear to you. Move the mixture to a medium mixing bowl.

5. In another different bowl, add the leftover 20 percent gluten-free oats.

6. Place the prawns in both the blended oats, the egg, and the blended oats.

7. Finally, put the prawns in the oats, which are not blended.

8. Place the chips on the grill pan and extract them from the air fryer.

9. Place the rest of the prawns in the air-fryer grill pan and allow them to cook at 360-degree F.

10. With fresh lemon juice, season the cooked prawns and chips.

11. Just serve.

28. Gambas 'Pil Pil' with Sweet Potato

Prep + Cook Time: 35 minutes | Servings: 3-4

Ingredients:

- 12 King prawns

- 4 garlic cloves

- 1 red chili pepper, de-seeded

- 1 shallot

- 4 tbsp. olive oil

- Smoked paprika powder

- 5 large sweet potatoes

- 2 tbsp. olive oil

- 1 tbsp. honey

- 2 tbsp. fresh rosemary, finely chopped

- 4 stalks lemongrass

- 2 limes

Directions:

1. Clean the prawns and gut them.

2. Perfect the garlic and red chili pepper, and chop the shallots.

3. To form a marinade, combine the red chili pepper, garlic, and olive oil alongside the paprika. Let the prawns marinate in the marinade for approximately 2 hours.

4. By cutting the sweet potato, make perfect slices. Using 2 tablespoons of olive oil, honey, and chopped rosemary to mix the potato slices. Inside of an air fryer, bake the potatoes at 360-degree F for 15 minutes.Thread the prawns onto the lemongrass stalks when baking the potatoes. Increase the temperature to 390-degree F, and the prawn skewers are also included.Allow 5 minutes to cook the mixture.

Serve alongside wedges of lime.

29. Fried Hot Prawns with Cocktail Sauce

Prep + Cook Time: 20 minutes | Servings: 4

Ingredients:

- 1 tsp chili powder

- 1 tsp chili flakes

- ½ tsp freshly ground black pepper

- ½ tsp sea salt

- 8-12 fresh king prawns

For Sause:

- 1 tbsp. cider or wine vinegar

- 1 tbsp. ketchup

- 3 tbsp. mayonnaise

Directions:

1. Ensure that your Air Fryer is set to 360-degree F.

2. Get a clean bowl and combine the spices in it.

3. Coat the prawns by tossing them in the spice's mixture.

4. Transfer the spicy prawns into the air fryer basket and place the basket in the air fryer.

5. Allow the prawns to cook for 6 to 8 minutes (how long depends on the size of the prawns).

6. Get another clean bowl and make a mixture of the sauce ingredients.

7. Serve the prawns while hot alongside the cocktail sauce.

30. Crispy Air-fryer Coconut Prawns

Prep + Cook Time: 25 minutes | Servings: 2

Ingredients:

- 1 lb. fresh prawns

- 3 oz. granola

- 1 tbsp. Chinese five-spice

- 1 tbsp. mixed spice

- 1 tbsp. coriander

- Salt and ground black pepper to taste

- 1 lime rind and juice

- 2 tbsp. light coconut milk

- 3 tbsp. desiccated coconut

- 1 small egg

Directions:

1. After cleaning your prawns, lay them out on a chopping board.

2. Blend the granola in a blender until it appears like fine breadcrumbs.

3. Before removing the granola blend from the blender, add all the seasonings, lime, and coconut mix.

4. Whizz the blender around again.

5. Get a clean bowl and beat your egg in it using a fork.

6. While holding each prawn by the tail, dip it into the egg and the batter one after another.

7. After dipping all the prawns line the baking sheet at the bottom of the air fryer with your prawns.

8. Allow cooking at 360-degree F for 18 minutes.

9. Serve the cooked prawns.

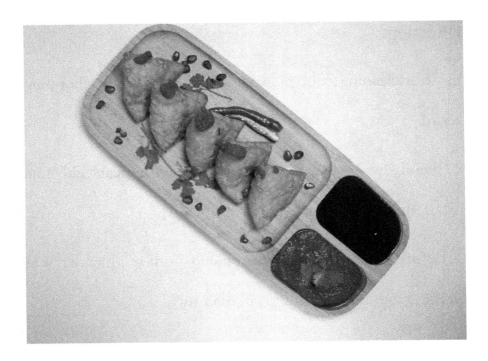

Chapter 12. Home Bakery Recipes

31. Cornish Pasty Recipe

Prep + Cook Time: 45 minutes | Servings: 4

Ingredients:

- 1 large carrot, peeled and sliced into small cubes

- 1 medium potato, peeled and sliced into small cubes

- 0.5 lb. plain flour

- 4 oz. butter

- 2 to 3 tbsp. water (cold)

- 4 oz. minced pork

- 1 tbsp. olive oil

- 1 tsp mixed herbs

- Salt and ground black pepper to taste

- 1 tsp thyme

- 1 small egg, beaten

Directions:

1. In a food steamer, cause the carrot and potato to cook for 20 minutes or until tender. Set the cooked vegetables aside.

2. Create the pastry until you have a breadcrumb appearance by rubbing the butter into the flour. Apply a little cold water intermittently to achieve a good fluffy dough. Prepare the pastry for the Cornish pasties to come out.

3. Get a big pan and blend the mince in it with a little olive oil. Cook the mixture until it has stopped browning. Then add the steamed potato, seasoning, and carrot. Thoroughly blend again and stock separately.

4. Cover, generously, half of one side of the Cornish pastry with a cold filling.

5. Brush the egg with the pastry.

6. Move the pastry to the air fryer.

7. Enable for 25 minutes to cook at 400-degree F, or until the pastry is baked to your satisfaction.

8. Remove and serve.

Chapter 13. Rice Recipes

32.   Sticky Mushroom Rice

Prep + Cook Time: 25 minutes | Servings: 6

Ingredients:

- 16 oz. jasmine rice, uncooked

- 4 tbsp. maple syrup

- 2 tsp Chinese 5 Spice

- 4 tbsp. rice vinegar or white wine

- ½ cup soy sauce, you can use gluten-free tamari

- ½ tsp ground ginger

- 4 cloves garlic, finely chopped

- 16 oz. Cremini mushrooms wiped clean (any other mushrooms cut in half)

- ½ cup peas, frozen

Directions:

1. Store your cooked rice separately.

2. Combine the maple syrup, rice vinegar, soy sauce, ground ginger, garlic, and 5 Chinese spices in a clean dish.

3. Make sure the air fryer is preheated to 350-degree F.

4. In an air fryer, cause the mushrooms to cook for 10 minutes.

5. Open an air fryer after 10 minutes and shake or stir the mushrooms.

6. Pour the liquid mixture over the mushrooms that have been roasted, followed by the peas.

7. Stir and boil for an additional 5 minutes.

8. Finally, add the cooked hot rice to the mushroom sauce and stir well.

9. Serve.

Chapter 14. Beans and Legumes Recipes

33. Falafel

Prep + Cook Time: 1 d 1 h 45 m | Servings: 15

Ingredients:

- 1 cup dry garbanzo beans

- 1 clove garlic

- 1 small red onion, quartered

- 3/4 cup fresh flat-leafed parsley, stems removed

- 1 ½ cups fresh cilantro, stems removed

- 1 tbsp. ground cumin

- 1 tbsp. Sriracha sauce

- 2 tbsp. chickpea flour

- 1 tbsp. ground coriander

- Salt and ground black pepper to taste

- ¼ tsp baking soda

- ½ tsp baking powder

- Cooking spray

Directions:

1. Loosen and remove the skin after soaking the chickpeas in water for 24 hours by rubbing them with your fingertips. The skin-less chickpeas are rinsed and drained, and spread on a big, clean dish towel. This will cause them to dry up.

2. In a food processor, mix the garlic, onion, parsley, cilantro and chickpeas and blend until you have a rough paste. In a large bowl, pour the mixture into it.

3. Toss the cumin, Sriracha salt, chickpea flour, coriander, salt and pepper into the bowl containing the blended mixture. Before covering the mug, combine thoroughly. For 1 hour, let the mixture rest.

4. Ensure your air fryer is preheated to 375-degree F.

5. Before thoroughly mixing with your hands to ensure even blending, apply baking soda and baking powder to the chickpea mixture. Mold the mixture into 15 equal-sized balls, softly pressing each ball to create patties. With cooking sauce, spray the patties.

6. Arrange seven falafel patties in the basket of the air fryer and give 10 minutes to cook.

7. Remove the cooked falafel and place them on a plate.

8. Do the same for the other eight falafels, cooking for 10-12 minutes

Chapter 15. Pasta Recipes

34.   Maccaroni and Cheese Mini Quiche Recipe

Prep + Cook Time: 30 minutes | Servings: 4

Ingredients:

- Shortcrust pastry

- 1 tsp garlic puree

- 2 tbsp. Greek yogurt

- 8 tbsp. leftover macaroni and cheese

- 2 large eggs, beaten

- 12 oz. whole milk

- Grated cheese, optional

Directions:

1. Rub the bottom with some flour when washing your ramekin.

2. On the bottom of the ramekin, pass the short crust pastry.

3. Get a small, clean bowl and mix the garlic, Greek yogurt and the unused macaroni in it.

4. Cover the ramekins (up to 3/4 full) with the yogurt and garlic mixture.

5. Grab a separate bowl and combine the milk and eggs. Pour the paste over the cheese with the macaroni.

6. Make sure the air fryer is preheated to 355-degree F.

7. Load the cheese onto the ramekins as toppings and pass them to the air fryer.

8. Enable them to cook for 20 minutes.

9. Remove and serve.

Chapter 16. Potato Recipes

35.   Garlic and Parsley Baby Potatoes

Prep + Cook Time: 30 minutes | Servings: 4

Ingredients:

- 1 pound baby potatoes, cut into quarters

- 1 tbsp. avocado oil

- ¼ tsp salt

- ½ tsp granulated garlic

- ½ tsp dried parsley

Directions:

1. Make sure the air fryer is pre-heated to 350-degree F.

2. Add the potatoes and oil to a clean bowl.

3. Add 1/4 teaspoon of granulated garlic and 1/4 teaspoon of parsley and toss with the potatoes to cover. To coat, throw the potatoes again.

4. For the last time, add the remaining garlic, parsley, and salt and toss.

5. Switch the potatoes to the basket of the air fryer and allow to cook until golden-brown, while flipping at some point. This will take 20 to 25 minutes or so.

Chapter 17. Vegetables

36. Butternut Squash Roasties

Prep + Cook Time: 15 minutes | Servings: 2

Ingredients:

- 1 small butternut squash

- 2 tbsp. olive oil

- Mixed herbs chicken seasoning

- Salt and ground black pepper to taste

Directions:

1. Make sure the air fryer is preheated to 360-degree F.

2. Peel the squash with the butternut and dice it.

3. Throw it in the discarded mixed spice seasoning with the butternut squash drizzled in the olive oil.

4. Switch it to the air fryer, then.

5. Set the timer to 10 minutes and allow it to cook until you become golden in color.

6. Serve alongside herbs that are new.

37.   Avocado Fries

Prep + Cook Time: 35 minutes | Servings: 4

Ingredients:

- 1½ tsp ground black pepper

- ½ cup (about 2 1/8 oz.) all-purpose flour

- 2 large eggs

- 1 tbsp. water

- ½ cup panko (Japanese-style breadcrumbs)

- 2 avocados, cut into 8 wedges each

- Cooking spray

- ¼ cup no-salt-added ketchup

- 2 tbsp. canola mayonnaise

- 1 tbsp. apple cider vinegar

- 1 tbsp. Sriracha chili sauce

- ¼ tsp kosher salt

Directions:

1. Mix the pepper and flour together in a clean, shallow dish and stir thoroughly.

2. Grab another shallow dish and gently beat the eggs while adding water.

3. Placed the panko in the third shallow dish and set it aside.

4. Dip the avocado wedges into the flour and shake off the excess, then into the mixture of the egg, allowing any excess to run off, and eventually, when pressing to stick, dredge in the panko. Use the cooking spray to produce a generous coating on the avocado wedges.

5. Arrange the avocado wedges in the air-fryer basket and let cook at 400-degree F for 7-8 minutes. Turn them to cook halfway.

6. Meanwhile, to make the sauce, mix the ketchup, mayonnaise, vinegar, and Sriracha in a single, shallow dish.

7. Remove the fried wedges and dust with salt from the air fryer.

8. On each slice, serve four avocado fries alongside two tablespoons of the sauce.

39. Air Fried Guacamole

Prep + Cook Time: 5 hours 25 minutes | Servings: 10

Ingredients:

- 1 egg

- 1 egg white

- 1/3 cup almond flour (coconut flour; tapioca or arrowroot powder)

- 3 oz. gluten-free panko (regular panko; wheat breadcrumbs)

- Cooking spray olive oil

Guacamole:

- 3 medium ripe avocados

- 1/3 cup chopped onion

- Juice from 1 lime

- 2 tsp cumin

- Fresh finely chopped cilantro to taste (about 1/3 cup)

- Sea salt and ground black pepper to taste

- 8 tbsp. fine almond flour

Directions:

1. Get a clean bowl and mix all the guacamole ingredients, except the almond flour, in it and mash them.

2. Add the almond flour when the flavor is what you want before the guacamole gets as smooth as the brownie batter. In order to achieve the desired thickness, you can need to add extra tablespoons of almond flour. Add mild lime juice since the excess can just loosen and wet the guacamole. Put the bowl in the freezer and allow roughly 1-2 hours to harden. Remove until it has hardened the guacamole.

3. To cover a baking dish, use a non-stick foil or a parchment sheet. Scoop the hardened guacamole out and turn it into a ping pong ball the size of a ball. Move the guacamole-shaped ball to the baking tray. Do the same for the guacamole that remains.

4. Cover the non-stick foil with the tray and return to the fridge. Leave overnight or for a period of 4 hours.

5. Make sure the air fryer is preheated to 390-degree F.

6. Get a clean bowl and beat the eggs together in it.

7. You would need to operate here in clusters but at full speed. Lightly coat the guacamole ball with olive oil, then dip it in the almond flour until it is moist, then the egg mixture and eventually the panko crumbs. Until the air fryer basket is filled, do the same with the leftover guacamole balls. Be sure to leave breathing space in the basket between the balls. Both balls that are uncoated should be returned to the freezer.

8. In an air fryer, position the basket and spray with a little olive oil.

9. Set the timer for 6-8 minutes and allow to cook until golden brown emerges on the outside. Remove them from the air fryer as the balls start cracking. Just return them when they're cold and firmer.

10. Now coat the uncoated balls and air-bake them.

11. Serve and enjoy.

Chapter 18: Dessert Recipes

40. Chocolate Cupcakes with Cream Cheese Frosting Recipe

Prep + Cook Time: 25 minutes | Servings: 8

Ingredients:

- ¼ of the mixture chocolate cake batter

- 3 oz. butter

- 9 oz. brown sugar

- 14 oz. soft cheese

- 1 tbsp. vanilla essence

- 3 tbsp. organic cocoa powder

Directions:

1. The first step is to make the cake batter – simply mix it like you were making a chocolate cake. Set aside when ready.

2. Get eight small cupcake cases. Flour the base of each, as well as the sides. This prevents them from getting sticky.

3. Pour in the cake batter into each of the cases until they are ¾-filled.

4. Transfer them into the air fryer and allow cooking at 400 degree F for 7 minutes.

5. To make the cream frosting, combine the butter, brown sugar, soft cheese, and vanilla in a clean mixing bowl. Use a hand mixer to mix until the mixture is creamy and smooth.

6. Transfer the frosting into the freezer and leave for an hour. This makes it firm up a bit.

7. With the aid of the cake decorating kit, add ¼ of the set frosting cake into the cake decorator.

8. Using a fork, mix the cocoa powder in the bowl until the mixture appears nice and chocolate in color.

9. Add the rest of the mixture into the cake decorating kit, and swirl the cupcake layer right on the top of the buns.

10. Keep the buns in the fridge for 20 minutes before serving.